In
TV NEWS

DEBORAH FOX

EVANS BROTHERS LIMITED

Published by Evans Brothers Limited
2a Portman Mansions
Chiltern Street
London
W1M 1LE

First published in 1998

Commissioned by: Su Swallow
Design: Neil Sayer
Photographer: Gareth Boden
Illustrator: Liam Bonney/The Art Market

British Library Cataloguing in Publication Data

Fox, Deborah
  People at work in TV news
  1.Television broadcasting of news - Juvenile literature
  I.Title
  791.4'5655

ISBN 0237518228

Printed in Hong Kong by Wing King Tong

Acknowledgements

The author and publisher wish to thank the following for their
help:
Phil Evans, Fiona MacEachin, Sheila Jansen and the newsroom
and staff of Sky News.

The following photographs are reproduced with the kind
permission of Sky News: pages 22(top) and 27 (top).

Contents

The news presenter   8

The news desk   10

Covering the story   12

In the studio   14

In the gallery   16

On air   18

The video package   20

Cut to the live interview   22

Business and sports presenters   24

Preparing for the next day   26

Glossary   28

Index   29

The news presenter

My name is Sheila and I am a presenter for a television news channel, where news is broadcast live to millions of viewers for 24 hours a day, every day of the year. I start work at 8 o'clock in the morning when I go straight into make-up. Then I have about an hour to brief myself on the stories that have broken and the interviews I will be doing.

Going in to make-up every morning is a necessary part of the job. It is vital to look your best on air.

▲ *The news team discuss the news stories that have broken. They decide which stories should be featured in our news programmes.*

Editorial meetings

Working on live television is exciting. A news story will break and we can put it on air within a few minutes. Every morning the Head of News holds editorial meetings with executive producers and news editors to decide which stories we will cover and which shall be our lead, or top, stories.

After university I did a graduate training course with a TV station. I worked in regional news for three years as a reporter. I moved to another regional news station where I got some experience as a presenter. Most news presenters are trained journalists.

The news desk

Home and foreign news is fed through to the news desk. The team of people who work here collect all the up-to-date news and the news editor decides which stories the reporters should follow up.

News from all over the world is gathered by a team of people who work on the news desk. The team collects the news from a wide range of sources; for example, special news services and agencies send new stories to TV and radio stations and newspapers. The news desk team also watches other TV stations, reads all the newspapers and listens to radio news. There are hundreds of stories happening all over the world, and the job of the news editor is to decide which stories we should cover in the news programmes and how we should cover them. There are news editors for home news and for foreign news.

The executive producer

The executive producer turns the raw news provided by the news desk into our news programmes, deciding which stories the programmes should 'lead', or start, with. He talks to the news desk team about the stories he would like to feature and which stories are being covered.

▼ The executive producer might have strong ideas on which stories he would like to cover in detail and so he discusses them with the news editor.

I have a team of producers who report to me and they are responsible for individual programmes. The executive producer decides on content and the producer shapes it into a news programme.

Johnathan, executive producer

I like the fact that the job is so immediate and so unpredictable. You never know what is going to happen.

Rob, home news editor

Covering the story

I enjoy the excitement of being a reporter. You never know from one day to the next which stories you are going to cover. I also get the chance to travel to different countries.

Emma, general news reporter

▼ Karen, the reporter, is working on a story about a new car. She is being filmed for her report.

The news editors decide which stories the reporters should cover. The reporters can be sent anywhere in the world, or they may cover a local story. Reporters have to make sure they check all the facts of the story and talk to the right people. It is up to them to set up interviews. They have to make sure the report is interesting and informative.

▲ Karen has set up an interview with an editor of a new car magazine. She will include the interview in her report.

▽ The reporter writes up all the main points of the story.

The film crew

The camera operator is responsible for filming the report and the sound technician records the voices. When the reporter gets back to the office, she has to write up the report quickly for the news programme. Reporters have to work fast and to deadlines. With 24-hour news, the news is broadcast round the clock.

I love television because you can get more personality into it. I report on fashion and lifestyle stories, which are very visual. I can suggest new stories to my executive producer.
Karen, fashion and lifestyle correspondent

In the studio

It is about an hour before I go on air and so I look through the running order of the programme. The running order is a list of all the items and stories that will be covered in the programme with the amount of time each item will have. The producer for each programme produces the running order. I have a live interview and I prepare my questions and make sure that I am fully briefed on the news background to the interview. As a trained reporter, I know how important this is.

Just before I go in to the

▲ The make-up artist retouches my make-up in the studio before I go on air.

▶ I have a few minutes to look over the headlines and to check that everything is working properly.

news studio I attach my microphone. In front of me is a computer screen that gives me information on the main stories.

The floor manager

The floor manager keeps the studio running smoothly, letting me know how much time we have before we go on air and giving me any new stories

and scripts. We both talk to the director of the programme who lets the floor manager and myself know which camera I need to look at.

▲ The floor manager makes sure I have everything I need before we go out live.

In the gallery

"One minute, Sheila"

The director sits in the gallery. It is called a gallery because the array of screens is like a gallery of pictures. The different screens show all the visual sources the director has for the news programme. One screen shows me, the news presenter, other screens show the different videotape recordings we have, and another the scene of a live interview. During the course of the programme the director will cut to all these different sources and so everything needs to be clearly displayed.

The gallery team

The director's assistant keeps time with a stopwatch so that she can let the director know exactly how much time they have left on each item. The vision mixer watches the screens and fades or cuts from one source to another at exactly the right moment.

Talkback

Directors have to talk to a wide range of people at the same time. They use a system called 'talkback'. They talk into the microphone and the messages are relayed to the news presenter, the floor manager, the people who run the videotapes, the camera operator, the sound and lighting teams and the crews on location. The director is the coordinating voice, making sure everyone knows what is happening.

▲ Every second is vital so that the programme does not overrun. There is a large clock in the gallery and next to it a countdown of how much time is left until the end of the programme.

My job is to make sure the programme the producer wants is delivered in the right way, on time and with no mistakes. I work closely with the producer as I am putting all the visual stories together. A good news director will think around the running order too in case anything goes wrong. So if a tape isn't ready in time, the director has a Plan B and can suggest to the producer that they should rearrange the running order slightly.

Neil, director

▲ The director coordinates the programme and communicates using 'talkback'.

On air

▲ The lead-ins are clearly displayed on the autocue. I also have my script as a back-up.

It's important to keep your cool when you are working on live news. Things do go wrong and so you have to be able to think on your feet and explain that there is a problem. Sometimes a tape might not work or the autocue sticks, but luckily this doesn't happen very often!

Ten seconds to on air ... 3,2,1. "Good morning and welcome to ... " I read from the autocue in front of the camera. This means I don't have to keep looking at my script. I can look at the camera and keep eye contact with the viewer, which is really important.

First of all I read the lead-ins, which are introductions to the main news stories of the day. The producers write the lead-ins and they aim to give the viewers an overview of the main news and what we will be covering in the programme.

Taking a break

After I have read the lead-ins and focused on the main story of the programme, the director tells me through my earpiece that we have a video to run on that story. This means I have a break of a minute and a half. As the video report comes to an end, the director's assistant counts down from ten seconds to cue me in to the next story.

On the autocue

- **vtr** videotape recording.
- **lvo** live voice over. When images are shown and the news presenter talks over the images.
- **throwback** when another presenter, for example the sports presenter, hands back the audience to the main news presenter.

▼ The camera operator moves the camera by computer. The director tells the camera operator which camera to use and the camera operator makes sure it is correctly positioned.

The video package

The director tells me that we have another video report to run which will be on air for two minutes. The reporters who cover the daily stories produce the videotape reports, known as 'packages', with editors. When the reporters have finished filming their stories and have done their interviews, they have to produce the final version of the report. They produce a package that is informative, interesting and exactly the right length for the news programme.

Sometimes the editor chooses the best pictures and the reporter records the commentary later.

The edit suite

Working with an editor in a room called an edit suite, the reporter and editor cut out pieces of the film that are not usable and concentrate on the visual images they need to

tell the story. When out on location the camera operator might have shot up to 40 minutes of film, but there will only be time for about 45 seconds on the news programme! The reporter and editor have to choose the best images for those 45 seconds.

▲ *The reporter records her story on the new car that was filmed earlier in the day.*

In the edit suite

- **slug** *the name of the item being edited*
- **ss** *still shot, not a moving image*
- **soundbite** *5 or 10 seconds from an interview that sums up what a person thinks*

Recording the commentary

The reporters record their stories in the edit suite. Their words – the commentary – have to fit with the pictures. If film crews need to work overseas, they travel with an editor and send packages back to the main news studio.

An editor's job is to make the best pictures of the day tell the story. Editors have a good eye for pictures.

Robert, editor

Cut to the live interview

LIVE

The film crew film the politician on location. The viewer sees him, and the presenter in the studio, at the same time.

After the video report I cut to a live interview with a politician. I had about an hour earlier this morning to prepare the questions as the interviews are very much my own. It's important not to make the questions too complicated. I ask the questions that the viewers would like to ask. I have two minutes for the interview.

"Good morning. Could I start by asking you ..."

The graphics team

If producers or reporters want a specific photograph for their report they go to the graphics department. The graphics team can contact the stills library, which is stocked

Producers and reporters discuss what they need with the graphic designers.

with thousands of photographs, and they can call up the photograph on their computer screens. If producers or reporters want a caption to go with the photograph or simply the name of the person next to it, they tell the graphics designer what they would like and the words are typed in by the designer.

Using an electronic pen and pad the designers can change colours of images on the screen. If the colours of a photograph are a little bit dull, they can brighten them by using the

> You have to be quite creative and you have to work fast. The producer or reporter will request pictures and you have to decide how to present those pictures on the TV screen.
>
> Catherine, graphic designer

'paintbox' on their computer. The designers may have only a few minutes to get hold of a photograph that a producer wants for the next news bulletin. They have to work quickly and be sure that they have put the right words with the images.

▼ *The producer has an item on the Oscar film awards and so the graphic designer has to produce still images for the report.*

Business and sports presenters

I come in at 5am and find out what has happened in the business markets around the world. By about 6.30 we have most of what we need for the morning and then it is a question of reacting as and when things happen. I may need to ad lib if a story breaks. I may have to react to it straightaway, which is quite exciting. My shift ends at 2pm.

Mark, business presenter

"Biz throw." The autocue tells me that it is time to introduce the business presenter as he has just under four minutes to present the latest business news. The business presenter gives a report on how house prices have risen and what the forecast is for the next six months.

▼ The business reporter comes in to the studio about five minutes before he goes on air to go through the scripts.

Sports throw

▲ The sports presenter checks that he can hear the director clearly through his earpiece.

"And back now to Sheila," says the business presenter.
I look into Camera 3 again with the last news story of the day and the last taped report. During the tape the sports presenter comes into the studio with the latest sports news.

▼ Checking the sports headlines

On the autocue

- **sports or biz throw** term used to tell the main news presenter to introduce the sports or business presenter.
- **wrap** main headlines; a snapshot of the top stories, lasting about 15 to 20 seconds.

Preparing for the next day

▼ The newsroom buzzes all day and night as people work on new stories from around the world.

"That brings us to the end of the news. From the team, good afternoon."

With those words I end my news presenting for the day. Before going home I spend some time talking to the executive producer of the morning's programmes to ask how he thinks everything went.

▼ The newsroom buzzes all day and night as people work on new stories from around the world.

At the end of the programme the director moves to the weather presenter and the forecast for the UK and the rest of Europe.

TONIGHT

When I go home I make sure I stay on top of the news for the rest of the day so that I am prepared for the next day.

On some days I have only a half-hour break and so it is nice to relax with a paper.

Glossary

ad lib to make up on the spot; to talk openly without a prepared script

autocue a machine that is placed in front of the TV camera so that news presenters can read a script while looking at or towards the camera

break (when a story breaks) when a new story comes out; a fresh story

(to) brief to give someone information; to find out

broadcast to transmit or put out sounds or images by radio or television

bulletin summary or snapshot of the day's news

commentary the recorded words that go with a story

cue instruction to a presenter to start or stop speaking

earpiece tiny device that fits into the ear allowing the presenter to listen to instructions from the director, director's assistant or producer

edit suite the room where the tape editor puts together all the pictures in order to tell the story

gallery the studio control room

news agency an organisation that has its own team of reporters; it sells its news reports to newspapers, magazines and broadcasting companies

news station news broadcasting company

on air being broadcast; live

round the clock every minute of every day

script the words that the presenter reads out, with details of the camera shots and what graphics and videos will be shown

slug the title or name of the item being edited

soundbite a spoken summary lasting five or ten seconds

Index

autocue 18, 24, 25, 28

bulletin 10, 13, 23, 28
business presenter 24, 25

camera operator 17, 19
camera operator (on location) 13, 21
computers 15, 19, 23

deadlines 13
director 15, 16, 17, 18, 19, 20, 25, 28
director's assistant 16, 19, 28

earpiece 19, 25, 28
editorial meetings 9
editors 20, 21, 28
edit suite 20, 21, 28

fashion 13
film crew 13, 17, 21, 22
floor manager 15, 17
foreign news 10, 26

gallery 16-17, 28

graphics 17, 22-23

headlines 14, 25

interviews 8, 12, 13, 14, 16, 20, 21, 22

lead-ins 18, 19
live voice over 19
local news 12

make-up 8, 14
microphone 15, 17

news agencies 10, 28
news editors 9, 10, 11, 12
newspapers 10, 28

overseas reports 21

packages 20, 21
photographs 22-23
producers 11, 14, 17, 18, 22, 23, 28

radio 10, 28
reporters 10, 12, 13, 14, 20, 21, 22, 23, 28

running order 14, 17

scripts 15, 18, 28
slug 21, 28
soundbite 21, 28
sound technician 13
sports presenter 19, 25
stills library 22
studio 14, 15

talkback 17
throwback 19
timing 16, 17, 19

video report 19, 20
videotape 16, 17, 18, 19, 20
viewers 18, 22
vision mixer 16

weather 27
wrap 25